RISKY BUSINESS

Smokejumper

Firefighter from the Sky

By

KEITH ELLIOT GREENBERG

With Photography by Bill Moyer

A BLACKBIRCH PRESS BOOK

WOODBRIDGE, CONNECTICUT

Published by Blackbirch Press, Inc.
260 Amity Road
Woodbridge, CT 06525

Email: staff@blackbirch.com
Web site: www.blackbirch.com

©1995 Blackbirch Press, Inc.
First Edition

Printed in Hong Kong

10 9 8 7 6 5 4 3

Library of Congress Cataloging-in-Publication Data

Greenberg, Keith Elliot.
    Smokejumper/by Keith Greenberg. — 1st ed.
      p.   cm. — (Risky business)
    Includes bibliographical references and index.
    ISBN 1-56711-153-X (lib. bdg.)
    1. Smokejumping—Juvenile literature. 2. Williams, Wayne G.—
Juvenile literature. 3. Smokejumpers—United States—Juvenile literature.
[1. Williams, Wayne G. 2. Smokejumpers. 3. Forest fire fighters.]
I. Title. II. Series: Risky business (Woodbridge, Conn.)
SD421.23.G74   1995
634.9'618'092—dc20
[B] 363. 37   94-23658
                                                   CIP
                                                   AC

INTRODUCTION

In July 1940, the fire in Idaho's Nez Perce National Forest was raging. There were no roads cutting through the rugged timberland. To reach the flames, firefighters would either have to hike miles through the woods, or bring supplies by mule team. The battle against this disaster seemed hopeless.

On July 12, however, a new firefighting method was used. On that day, firefighters parachuted from an airplane into the forest. By using airplanes, these firefighters—called "smokejumpers"—saved valuable time and rescued hundreds of acres of precious wildland.

3

"Smokejumping has always attracted a different type of person," says Wayne Williams, a smokejumper from Missoula, Montana. "Some of the first smokejumpers were stuntmen. These were guys who performed at air shows, walking on the wings of the planes. Other people were afraid of using an airplane to jump *into* a fire. But these guys understood it was the fastest way to get the job done. Their attitude really separated them from everyone else. Even the military used their parachutes only as a last resort."

Wayne Williams is a smokejumper from Missoula, Montana.

Wayne rides his bike to
work as part of his daily
routine.

Staying in top physical condition is an important part of being a smokejumper. Wayne has worked hard all his life to stay fit. Since high school, he has raced bicycles, ran track, and played football. Upon graduating from Homestead High School in Sunnyvale, California, he began training as a firefighter for the California Division of Forestry.

Smokejumpers must stay
in top physical condition.

To be a smokejumper candidate, Wayne would have to get used to extreme conditions. "When you're fighting a fire, you can work for 24 hours straight," says Gary Benavidez, superintendent of the Missoula Smokejumper Base. "Every part of your body hurts. You have to push your body, then push it a little bit more."

During his firefighter training, Wayne stayed in a 100-person barracks in Angel's Camp, California. One of his first tasks was using a chain saw and hand tools to create a "fire line." A fire line is a trench built to surround a fire and prevent it from spreading.

Sometimes fighting fires means working around the clock.

In July 1974, Wayne was sent to a fire in Tahoe National Forest that smokejumpers could not reach.

"We got there about dark and got the fire out at 3 AM," Wayne remembers. With the flames out, he slept for three hours. When he woke up, he began "mopping up"—or putting out whatever burning embers remained. "We were on our hands and knees, digging up the ground, mixing dirt with the ash. Then we felt the ground to make sure there was no more fire."

 Firefighters often have to dig up dirt and mix it with ash to make sure a fire is completely out.

Smokejumper trainees prepare for a practice jump at the base in Missoula, Montana.

Wayne says that training at the base in Missoula "was as close as you could get to doing the real thing without doing it." There, he dove from a tower and hung from a platform as if he were caught in a tree.

There were also nine training jumps from actual planes. "You start off jumping into big spots of land, and then it gets smaller and smaller," Wayne says. "The eighth jump was into a tree. The ninth jump was into water."

Smokejumpers must work with a great deal of special equipment, including helmets, parachutes, and axes.

As he trained, Wayne was also put under tremendous physical pressure. During one drill, he worked from 3 PM, through the night, until 7 AM, digging a ditch for a practice fire line. Throughout the 13 hours, there were only two breaks for meals. Then, after breakfast, trainees put 100 pounds of weight on their backs and hiked for 3 miles.

When he received his first official smokejumping assignment, he was fully equipped. He had a shirt and pants made of flame-resistant Nomex material, chaps made of fireproof Kevlar, leather gloves, boots, and a hardhat

14

with an attached headlamp. In addition to a walkie-talkie, he carried a shovel and a "pulaski"—a curved axe designed for carving out fire lines.

In case the fire came too close, Wayne had a vinyl bag containing a small tent made of aluminum foil bonded on fiberglass. The shelter—large enough for only one person—quickly folds out and reflects off as much heat as 1,600 degrees. Inside, the temperature never rises above 200 degrees—uncomfortable, but no more dangerous than a dry sauna.

Wayne shows how his fireproof tent works.

Today, there are between 350 and 400 U.S. smokejumpers. Fifteen of them are women. All smokejumpers work out of 11 bases in the western United States.

Most smokejumpers are on call during "fire season," which are the summer months when the sun dries out plants and grass. During this dry time— when lightning strikes or campfires often burn unchecked—fires can start quickly.

Helicopters are often used to deliver water to a fire.

16

Smokejumpers can't do their job alone. They work with "smokechasers," who are the first to hike to the site of the fire. Helicopter crews can also dump thousands of gallons of water carried through the air in a large bucket.

Smokejumpers reach dangerous fires by parachuting into areas that cannot be reached in other ways.

A typical smokejumping operation has 16 people. Besides a pilot and co-pilot, there's a "spotter," who finds a good place for jumpers to land. He or she throws streamers out of the plane to test wind directions.

Two jumpers usually leave the airplane at a time. Then, the spotters toss down food, water, and tools.

A special firefighting chemical is often dropped from a plane onto the fire. It is red, so the smokejumpers can tell where it is before they parachute down.

Pilots, co-pilots, and spotters are important people in any mission.

Surprisingly, Wayne does not think of fire as an enemy. "We actually need fire for healthy forests," he explains.

When lightning strikes, fires burn. Once these blazes burn out, the ash actually helps to fertilize the soil. New plants can then grow, and wildlife returns to feed on the new resources.

As it burns, fire eats up oxygen in the air, creating white smoke. A gust of wind can then bring new oxygen in, erupting an area into flames.

"Fire is a living thing," Wayne says. "It does everything humans do. It breathes. It reacts to weather. It lives and dies."

One memorable blaze took place in 1992 at Nez Perce National Forest in Idaho. A 2-acre fire spread to 8,000 acres within 24 hours, due to heavy winds. In addition, Wayne and the other firefighters had to protect a house right in the middle of the blaze.

Overhead, a special helicopter crew assisted by releasing 2,000 pounds of water onto the flames.

During the fire, Wayne somehow got separated from the others. "I was surrounded by a bunch of fire," he says.

"Finally, the fire went burning off in different directions, and we saved the house. The family living there threw a party for us. It was great."

Smokejumpers create fire lines to stop the spread of a large fire.

A firefighter digs a fire line into the ground.

23

The 1994 fire season was one of the worst in recent years. Usually, fires begin in New Mexico and Arizona during May and June. Then, later, others start in Oregon, Washington State, Montana, and Idaho. California usually experiences its biggest fires in the fall.

In 1994, all these areas "were burning at once," as Wayne explains it. "The rains didn't come, and there were lightning fires everywhere. Every day, we were going from one fire to another."

During the 1994 season, smokejumpers faced very dry conditions and many fires.

During some years, smokejumpers work from spring through fall, fighting one fire after another.

25

For all the triumphs, there are also tragedies. Wayne's worst moment came at Canyon Creek in Colorado in July 1994. "Just as we got there the fire flew up. All the brush went up in flames."

Two smokejumpers work on finishing a fire line.

By the time the fire was put out, 3 smokejumpers and 11 other firefighters were dead. This was the greatest loss since 1949, when 12 smokejumpers died in Mann Gulch, Montana. Wayne is still haunted by his memory of counting the bodies while he searched for survivors.

"I never thought I'd see this," he says. "Now, I know that, no matter how hard we try to be safe, people can always die."

Wayne gets out of his suit after a long day.

Wayne helps a fellow smokejumper suit up.

Still, Wayne tries to keep bad thoughts out of his mind as he peddles his bicycle to work every day. At the base, he immediately updates himself on fires burning around the country. He always keeps a bag filled with clothing and equipment at the base in case he has to leave on a moment's notice.

"I can get called to any fire in the United States," he says. "One day, I came to work and thought I'd be home for dinner. Instead, I was sent across the country to North Carolina. One second, you can be sitting around at the base with nothing to do. Then, a horn blows and you're suiting up and running for a plane, on your way to a fire."

When he isn't fighting a blaze, Wayne inspects his parachute for rips and sews damaged equipment. He also goes to the gym regularly. All smokejumpers must do fitness training for an hour a day. "I'm paid to stay in shape," he says. "If I'm not in shape, I'm a bad investment."

Wayne works out as the parachutes are re-packed and loaded for use.

29

While others fear the idea of boarding an airplane for a distant forest, parachuting into a small spot, and fighting a violent fire, Wayne actually enjoys it.

"There's a closeness I feel with the other smokejumpers," he says. "We trust each other with our lives, and we like the people we work with. People say we're special, but I don't feel that way. The only thing special is that—unlike many other jobs—I look forward to going to work every day."

Smokejumpers are unique people who enjoy a life filled with tough challenges.

FURTHER READING

Conlon, Laura. *Fire*. Vero Beach, FL: Rourke, 1993.

Petty, Kate. *Fire*. New York: Franklin Watts, 1990.

Pringle, Laurence. *Fire in the Forest*. New York: Macmillian, 1993.

Seymour, Peter. *Fire Fighters*. New York: Dutton Children's Books, 1990.

INDEX